A ROOKIE BIOGRAPHY

ROBERT E. LEE

Leader in War and Peace

By Carol Greene

CHILDRENS PRESS®
CHICAGO

This book is for Sam Toole

Robert E. Lee (1807-1870)

Library of Congress Cataloging-in-Publication Data

Greene, Carol.
    Robert E. Lee : leader in war and peace / by Carol Greene
       p.   cm. — (A Rookie biography)
    Includes index.
    Summary: A simple biography of the general who commanded the
Southern Army during the Civil War.
    ISBN 0-516-04209-2
    1. Lee, Robert E. (Robert Edward), 1807-1870—Juvenile literature.
2. Generals—United States—Biography—Juvenile literature.
3. Confederate States of America. Army—Biography—Juvenile
literature. 4. United States. Army—Biography—Juvenile literature.
5. United States—History—Civil War, 1861-1865—Campaigns—Juvenile
literature. [1. Lee, Robert E. (Robert Edward), 1807-1870. 2. Generals.] I.
Title,
II. Series: Greene, Carol. Rookie biography.
E467.1.L4G74   1989
973.7'3'092—dc20
[B]
[92]   89-33749
                                                    CIP
                                                    AC

Robert E. Lee
was a real person.
He was born in 1807.
He died in 1870.
Lee was a great general
and a good man.
This is his story.

TABLE OF CONTENTS

George Washington, the first president of the United States of America, was one of Robert E. Lee's heroes.

Henry Lee, Robert's father, was born in 1756 and he died in 1818. When told of the death of George Washington, Henry Lee said Washington was "First in war, first in peace, and first in the hearts of his countrymen."

Chapter 1

Heroes

Young Robert E. Lee
had two heroes.
One was George Washington.
The other was
his own father, Henry Lee.

Both were fine soldiers.
Both were leaders.
Both tried to do their duty.

Washington died before
Robert was born.
But he had spent time
in Alexandria, Virginia,
where Robert lived.
Robert heard stories about him.

The Lee home, Stratford Hall, in Virginia

Henry Lee had fought
in the American Revolution.
He had been governor
of Virginia from 1791 to 1794.

But he was not
good at business.
He lost a lot of money.
He had to go to jail
until he could pay
his debts.

Henry Lee was nicknamed
"Light-Horse Harry" because
he led swift cavalry attacks
against the British.

Robert's mother, Anne Hill Carter Lee (above),
and his sister, Catherine Mildred (right)

Later, Henry Lee tried to help
a friend in a fight.
He was badly hurt.
He went away for five years
and tried to get well.

But when Robert was 11,
his father died.
Then his mother got sick.
His big brothers and sister
had all moved away.

Nursery (above) and a sitting room off the dining room (left) in Robert E. Lee's boyhood home. Stratford Hall in Westmoreland County, Virginia, is now a museum.

So Robert took care
of his mother
and helped run the house.
He also went to school.

Sometimes it was hard.
But Robert thought
about his heroes.
He must do his duty too.

Then one day,
Robert got a letter.
It said he could go
to West Point.

Robert was excited.
He thought about
his heroes again.
Now he could become
a soldier too.

West Point Military Academy on the Hudson River

Chapter 2

Jobs

Cadets at West Point
had to work hard.
They studied math,
science, drawing,
French, and more.
They marched every day.

Uniforms worn by the cadets at West Point

For four years,
Robert made good grades.
He made good friends too.
Then he joined the
Army Corps of Engineers.

Soon after that,
his mother died.
Robert missed her.
He said that he
"owed everything to her."

But he had a lot to do.
He worked on a fort
and other army jobs.

Painted in 1838, this portrait
shows Robert E. Lee in the dress uniform
of a lieutenant of engineers.

Mary Randolph Custis Lee (1808-1873)

He also got married.
He had known Mary Custis
for a long time.
Her grandfather was
the adopted son
of George Washington.

Robert and Mary
had seven children.
Robert loved his family.
But often he had to work
in other parts of the country.

Robert E. Lee's home (below),
now called Arlington House,
overlooks the Potomac River
and Arlington National
Cemetery. Certain rooms,
such as the parlor, are
open to the public.

In 1846 war broke out between Mexico and the United States. As a result of the war, Mexico gave up its land in Texas and most of the land in New Mexico, Arizona, California, Utah, and Nevada.

In 1846, he fought in a war
between the United States
and Mexico.
Soon everyone could see
what a fine soldier he was.

But Robert was kind too.
Once he stopped to help
a hurt Mexican boy.
He hated what war
could do to children.

Robert E. Lee after the Mexican War

When he came home again,
his own children were older.
They looked different.
Poor Robert hugged
a neighbor boy instead
of his son, Robert, Jr.

Next, the Army sent him
to be head of West Point.
That was a big job.
Then he worked
with the cavalry.
He had to travel again.

Years went by.
His children grew up.
Mary became crippled.
Robert felt sad now,
and much harder times
were coming.

Two of Lee's
daughters,
Eleanor Agnes
Lee (left)
and Mildred
Childe Lee (below)

In 1859 John Brown (below left) captured the arsenal at Harpers Ferry, Virginia (above). Brown thought that slaves from throughout the state would join him, but they didn't. Robert E. Lee led the troops that were sent to capture John Brown (below).

Chapter 3

A Hard Choice

In the middle of the 1800s,
people in the South
still owned slaves.
People in the North did not.
Many hated slavery.

In 1859, John Brown
attacked army buildings
in Harpers Ferry, Virginia.
He felt he was fighting
against slavery.

John Brown

21

John Brown is captured.

Lee was sent to stop him.
He arrested Brown.
Lee didn't like slavery either.
But he thought Brown
acted like a crazy man.

Abraham Lincoln was
elected president in 1860.
He asked Robert E. Lee
to take up a field command
in the Union army.

In 1860, Abraham Lincoln
was elected president.
States in the South
were not happy about that.
Some decided to form
their own nation.

Lee thought they were wrong.
He wanted the country
to be one nation.
But on April 12, 1861,
the Civil War began.

Robert E. Lee did not support slavery, but he did support the right of each state to be independent. Lee wrote ". . . I have not been able to make up my mind to raise my hand against my relatives, my children, my home. I have therefore resigned my commission in the army, and, save in defense of my native state—with the sincere hope that my poor services may never be needed—I hope I may never be called upon to draw my sword."

Lincoln asked Lee to be
head of the United States troops.
But Lee was from Virginia.
What was his real duty?
He thought hard.

Mary said that he
"wept tears of blood."
At last he chose
to go with Virginia.
Virginia chose to go
with the South.

In 1862, the governor
made Robert E. Lee
head of Virginia's army.
Now he was General Lee.
But he didn't want to fight.

Some people in the South
thought they would win quickly.
But Lee knew the war
would be terrible.
He did all he could
to get his troops ready.

Soon the soldiers learned
that war was terrible.
One man said it rained
for 32 days in August.
There wasn't enough food.
Many men got sick.

And the war had just begun.

Chapter 4

Terrible Years

The North had more
factories and soldiers
than the South.
But the South
had better generals.
Robert E. Lee was the best.

Traveller was
General Lee's
favorite
horse. This
photograph
was taken
in 1868 by
Michael Miley.

The Confederate soldiers
had a great love and respect
for Robert E. Lee.

At first the South
won many battles.
But thousands of soldiers
were killed or hurt.

Lee never forgot
that soldiers were people.
He did all he could for them.
"He looks after his men,"
said the soldiers.

The Confederate soldiers fought hard.
They believed they were fighting a
second war of independence.

Once a young prisoner
shouted at him,
"Hurrah for the Union!"
Lee looked at him.
The boy was hurt.
Lee got off his horse.

"Will he shoot me?"
wondered the boy.
But Lee held out his hand.
"My son," he said, "I hope
you will soon be well."

In 1863 at the bloody
battle at Gettysburg, Pennsylvania,
thousands of Union and
Confederate soldiers died.
General Lee did all he could,
but his soldiers were defeated.
This battle was the turning
point of the Civil War.

The terrible years went by.
Lee became head of
the whole Southern army.

But the South lost
more and more battles.
They were running
out of everything.

Many soldiers had no shoes.
Many had no food.
After a while,
there were no new soldiers
to take the place
of those who died.

Cities lay in ruins.
Railroads were blown up.
Crops were dead.
At last Lee knew that
the war must end.

A photograph of
the ruined city of
Richmond, Virginia,
taken in 1865.

9ᵗʰ Apᵉˡ '65—

Genᶫ I have recᵈ your note
of this date. Though not enter
-taining the opinion you express
of the hopelessness of further resis
-tance on the part of the Army
of N. Va.— I reciprocate your
desire to avoid useless effusion
of blood, & therefore before Consider
-ing your proposition ask
the terms you will offer— on
Condition of its Surrender—
Very respᵗ your Obᵗ Servᵗ
R E Lee
Genᶫ

Lt Genᶫ U. S. Grant
Commᵈ Armies of the U. States

General Robert E. Lee's note to General Grant
asking for the terms of surrender (left).
Generals Grant and Lee with their aides
met at McLean's house at Appomattox Court
House, Virginia (above), to sign the surrender.

After the papers were signed, General Lee
said farewell to General Grant, mounted Traveller,
and rode back to his soldiers.

He got on Traveller,
his big gray horse,
and rode to meet
the North's General Grant.
On April 9, 1865,
Robert E. Lee surrendered.

General Robert E. Lee says good-bye to his soldiers.

The next day,
he told his men
how brave they were.
He asked God to bless them.
Then he said good-bye.

Chapter 5

Peace

Lee rode home
to his family.
He felt old and sad
and very tired.

People in the South
had no money now.
Many had no jobs.
Some hated the North.

General Lee and his soldiers
return to their homes.

The war aged
Robert E. Lee.

Lee knew that was wrong.
He said that people
must forget the war.
They must work for peace.
Then their children
would have a better life.

The war took its toll on Mary Custis Lee, too.

Once he stopped
some children from beating
a Northern boy.
He took the boy
into his own house.

Another time, a black man
came to Lee's church.
He went to the front
to take communion.
That made people angry.

But Lee got up at once.
He went to the front
and knelt beside the man.
Soon everyone else
did the same thing.

Many people admired Lee.
They wanted to give him gifts.
A rich man said Lee could
have a big house in England
and all the money he needed.
But Lee loved Virginia.

A Mathew Brady photograph of Robert E. Lee

Then one day, a stranger
came to see him.
He was from Washington College
in Lexington, Virginia.
The college wanted Lee
to be its president.

Lee didn't know if
he could do that job.
His friends said he could.
So in September, 1865,
he rode Traveller
to his new home.

Lee became president of Washington College in Lexington, Virginia.

At first, the college
was in bad shape.
But Lee helped it grow.
One day it would become
Washington and Lee University.

The chapel (above) on the campus of
Washington College is now called the
Lee Chapel. The college was later
renamed Washington and Lee University
to honor Robert E. Lee.

Lee did a lot of work
for his church too.
One day he went
to a church meeting.
He walked home in the rain.

All at once,
he became very sick.
He couldn't even talk.
For days he lay in bed.
Sometimes he thought
he was back in the war.

Robert E. Lee died in this house.

Robert E. Lee was buried beneath the chapel (at right) on the campus of Washington College. Sometimes called "The Shrine of the South," thousands of people visit the Lee Chapel every year.

On October 12, 1870,
General Robert E. Lee
gave his last order.
"Strike the tent," he said.
(That means take it down.)
Then he died.

He had been a fine soldier.

He had been a leader.

He had done his duty.

For many people everywhere
he would always be a hero.

Important Dates

1807	January 19—Born in Westmoreland County, Virginia, to Henry and Ann Lee
1825-29	Went to United States Military Academy at West Point
1831	Married Mary Custis
1846-48	Fought in the Mexican War
1852-55	Was superintendent of West Point
1862	Became commander of Virginia's army
1865	Became general-in-chief of the South's armies Surrendered to Ulysses S. Grant Became president of Washington College
1870	October 12—Died at Lexington, Virginia

INDEX

Page numbers in boldface type indicate illustrations.

PHOTO CREDITS

ABOUT THE AUTHOR

Carol Greene has degrees in English Literature and Musicology. She has worked in international exchange programs, as an editor, and as a teacher. She now lives in St. Louis, Missouri, and writes full-time. She has published more than seventy books. Others in the Rookie Biographies series include *Benjamin Franklin*, *Pocahontas*, *Martin Luther King, Jr.*, *Christopher Columbus*, *Abraham Lincoln*, and *Ludwig van Beethoven*.